Green Golf Balls

Are you lost in the rough?

Daniel Schoepf

Cover photography: Lindsey Schoepf
Photo editor: Meghan Archer
Layout and design: Jason Buck

NICOLE,
YOU ARE NOT MEANT
TO BLEND IN

Green
Golf Balls

LIVE
TO

STAND OUT!

DON SCHNEPP
CHILD

ISBN: 1456584480
EAN-13: 9781456584481
LCCN: 2011901748

To Bill and Lucille Schoepf,
who taught me that anything is possible.

Contents

Foreword

Green Golf Balls is a simple concept that breaks down some of life's complexity. That is what makes it so powerful, memorable, and impactful. Life's lasting messages are the simplest: "Do unto others…," "Wash your hands," "Please," "Thank you." This book can be read quickly but it's not written for that. Read this book slowly. Reflect on the lessons. Don't rush through in a quick quest for self-improvement. The best way to absorb the lasting lessons is to read each chapter and take time to apply them. Write your answers in this book. This book was written to teach you. It was also written to test you. Absorb the lessons and make them active. You'll change your life.

CHAPTER 1

How to Find Out If You Are One

The only limits to the possibilities in your life tomorrow are the buts you use today.

Les Brown

Why aren't there any green golf balls? I was running by a golf course near our home one night and the idea of a green golf ball jumped in my head. It probably sliced in my head based on my actual golf game. It was getting dark and as I ran, I found myself hoping I would not sprain my ankle on a stray golf ball shanked directly in my running path. With more thought on the subject, I quickly decided that I would be able to see a traditional, white ball, and avoid stepping on it. Then I said a silent prayer, thankful nobody used Green Golf Balls.

At first, you may think Green Golf Balls would be unique. After all, how many Green Golf Balls have you seen? None? One? You have probably never seen one, and neither have I. There's a reason for that. They would be difficult to find after you hit them, even if they landed in the fairway (which mine rarely do). This characteristic flaw would kill the demand for the product. Even if they went where they were supposed to, what use would they have?

It hit me that too many people are like Green Golf Balls—they simply blend in. Even if they go where they're supposed to go (work, school, church, etc.) they get lost. When does this happen? Why does this happen? How does this happen? What can you do if it happens to you?

Upon further reflection, I realized that Kermit the Frog's musical wisdom was flawed. It **IS** easy being green. This may explain why so many people do it. It's easy. Let's explore a few of the courses taken by Green Golf Balls (GGB). One great way to determine your status as a GGB is to ask questions. Actually, that's only part of it. You must also answer them. Oh…and answer them honestly.

Tee these up and swing honestly.

➤ When was the last time you failed at something?

➤ Why did you fail?

➤ What could you have done differently to avoid the failure?

➤ What did you learn from it?

➤ Was this a mistake you have made once before or numerous times?

➤ Would you try it again?

➤ What was the last real life lesson you learned?

➤ How has it impacted your life?

➤ Have you taught anyone else this lesson?

➤ What have you always wanted to do in your life?

Lou Holtz was fired from his job and used the opportunity to write a list of 107 things he wanted to accomplish in his life. Many people (GGBs) would have been devastated and confused. Not Lou. He was determined and focused. Some of the goals he listed seemed preposterous at the time. He wanted to visit the White House. His wife wanted him to get a job. Both of these things happened and almost every goal listed was achieved. Determination and vision in spite of harsh realities? Powerful!

➤ What do you dream of doing someday?

➤ Why haven't you done it?

➤ Who would be disappointed that you didn't do it?

➤ How would you explain the disappointment or the dream to them?

➤ Where do you want to go in the world?

➤ How do you want your obituary heading to read?

Here are a few examples, and what you might take from them:

Physician was a pioneer
What can you lead? What can you pioneer? You're pioneering your family and life now. Where are you leading it?

A "diva" with a kind heart

No act of kindness ever disappears. Are you kind? Do you pay it forward? Are you a nice person?

Tennis was his passion

Do you even have a passion? If you have one, is it apparent? Do others know what it is? How are you pursuing your passion?

Fun-loving and involved

Ralph Waldo Emerson wrote, "It is a happy talent to know how to play." Do you have fun? Does it show? Do you encourage others to have fun?

A quiet community leader

What do you lead? Are you setting an example? Is it a good example?

He loved sports, travel

What do you truly, deeply, passionately, and unconditionally love? Who do you truly, deeply, passionately, and unconditionally love? What will you do immediately to prove it?

He had the "biggest heart"

It's ironic that my father had a faulty heart—only faulty in the physiological sense. In a caring sense, in a loving sense, in a giving sense, it was the strongest heart that ever pumped. If he wasn't at work or in the hospital, he was at one of our events or games. Would anybody think you had a "big heart"?

Family, church were first

There are many other things that GGBs put ahead of their family and church. Do you?

Promise is left unfulfilled

This was the headline for a twenty-seven-year-old that died in an automobile accident. Sometimes our plans are changed. They're always changed for the better...if you translate them that way. Is your promise unfulfilled?

A life defined by service

What is your life defined by? **Now** is what matters most. **Now** is what we have, nothing more, nothing less, but that's enough. What are we doing today? We're writing something. Every action, every smile, every frown, every meeting, every minute, every day, every week, month, and year we're writing something. It's the story of our life. What's yours? Will it say this?

He was a Green Golf Ball

Is this what you want your tombstone to say?

She was a Green Golf Ball

Really? Is this what you want?

If answering these questions seems like a waste of time because it won't change the path you're on...you're a GGB and destined to remain that way.

HOW TO FIND OUT IF YOU ARE ONE

➤ Ask questions and answer them honestly.

➤ Look ahead—what do you want written on your tombstone?

Summary

Tee these up!

One thing I will do to determine if I am a GGB after reading this chapter:

One thing I will continue to do after reading this chapter that will stop me from continuing as a GGB:

One thing I will start doing after reading this chapter that will help me determine my status:

CHAPTER 2

How You May Have Become One

Destiny is not a matter of chance, but of choice. Not something to wish for, but to attain.

William Jennings Bryan

When you're born, the possibilities are infinite. You start aging and the boundaries begin to constrict. With each year, you may *feel* as if your options are being reduced. When you become aware of your environment and surroundings, assimilation often occurs. Fear of standing out may overcome your desire for achievement. You want to fit in, so you pay attention to those you admire. It could be a sibling or parent or close friend. In a majority of cases, it is a Green Golf Ball that is selected to emulate. You begin to talk like he/she talks and emulate his/her behaviors. Green Golf Balls are often the parents and children of Green Golf Balls. The cycle is difficult to break. Conformity is a powerful force, powerful enough to keep people average or below. What follows is a very difficult question to answer honestly. Did you become a GGB because you selected the wrong role model? Is this how you became a GGB? Did you select the wrong role models? You can select new ones. Be careful.

Another reason people become Green Golf Balls is that they're in a family of them. They feel it is their destiny and that it has been pre-determined. They could make decisions to change their future, but one thing keeps them from doing it. Conformity feels so much better and aligns with human nature. It is easier and requires no discipline.

There are two pains in life. The pain of discipline is incurred daily. It is paid in the choices you make such as what you eat, how much you sleep, and what you think about.

The pain of regret is usually paid for all at once and painfully. The pain of regret and remorse is magnified by delay and inattention. GGBs pay the regret debt on a gurney as they're muttering, "I shouldn't have eaten all those bacon burgers." More often than not, Green Golf Balls do what they want to do or what they think others want them to do, or what they think is the right thing to do, or what they think will make others happy versus doing what they **should** do. It takes courage to overcome conformity, and one thing Green Golf Balls lack is the courage to move off the top of the bell curve.

The primary reason people end up being Green Golf Balls is a result of poor choices. Many GGBs turned green and remain green because they rely on circumstances as decision makers. At one point in time, something happened to them. It happened "to them" or at least that's what they deeply believe. It is this ingrained thought and perceived lack of control that keeps a *victim* of circumstance rather than a victor. They remain GGBs rather than victors. This event, whatever it is, often makes them bitter. GGBs prefer to let something or someone else define them and shape their thoughts. The people that avoid the GGB syndrome use events and circumstances to prepare them instead of…. GGBs use the event to close them up further and causing them to withdraw and take fewer risks, and it can drastically limit their growth. They keep this experience inside. Contrast that with non-GGBs. Non-GGBs use the event to open up even more and often share the experience to teach others. The same event could occur and a non-GGB would find a way for it to make them better.

The GGB would say, "It really set me back" or "cost me a lot" or "I'll never get over it." The non-GGBwould say, "It didn't kill me and it propelled me ahead." Or he/she might say, "That was a great lesson."

Another reason people become Green Golf Balls is the stigma of failure or the fear of failure. Just listen to a teenager talk with friends; the word "loser" is likely to be heard with regularity. Too few people dare to try something for fear of being called a "loser." They would rather be a Green Golf Ball and just blend in with the crowd. I believe that a "loser" is way better than a non-starter or someone that doesn't try and becomes a Green Golf Ball. Are you one?

The final reason people may become GGBs is that they lack the ability to adapt. At one time, they may have actually stood out academically, athletically, musically, or in some other field. Perhaps they were a star high-school football player, and the lights no longer shine on them; they live in the past and are unable to find another passion. Big Deal. The glory days are gone and hazy. The GGB can't salvage the positive aspects of their past success instead of recognizing how they can leverage their past heroics. The former star player had to work to stay on top. Why not pull work ethic out of that highlight reel? The star basketball player was not afraid to take the last shot and risk losing the game. Why not pull risk taking out of the pile of memories?

You may believe that non-GGBs only come from big cities. After all, they're exposed to more things and opportunity. Perhaps you believe the non-GGBs only come from wealthy families. They can buy opportunity, right?

They must come from big, famous states like California or New York or Texas. Sure they do, but non-GGBs can come from anywhere in the world. Is that true? Of course it is.

How you react to events in your life determine what happens next. Are you a victor or victim? Better or bitter? Do you persevere or perish? Do you learn or yearn? Does the experience define you or prepare you? Your responses to circumstances in your life have led you into the rough as a Green Golf Ball or straight down the middle of the fairway.

Wherever you are…right now…at this time…while you hold this book, you possess everything you need to be great.

HOW YOU MAY HAVE BECOME ONE

➤ You selected the wrong role models.

➤ You are in a family of them.

➤ You have made poor choices.

➤ The stigma of failure has conquered you.

➤ You have a lack of resiliency.

Summary

Tee these up!

One thing that may have contributed to becoming a Green Golf Ball:

One thing I will continue to do to keep from becoming a Green Golf Ball:

One thing I will start doing to shed my status as a Green Golf Ball:

CHAPTER 3

Why You Have to Stop Being One

We must make the choices that enable us to fulfill the deepest capacities of our real selves.

Thomas Merton

You owe it to your children. Are you a parent? Do you have aspirations of mediocrity for your children? Do you want them to become GGBs? Of course not. However, if you're a GGB, your children are likely to follow. Children emulate adults. This is scary. As a parent, you must set a good example, and living, acting, talking, and behaving like a GGB is not what you want your children to witness. Is it?

My father was not a GGB, not even close. At a distance, it's possible to think he may have been one. After all, he never made much money. He didn't perform incredible athletic feats. He didn't have a stellar career. He moved his family from California (swimming pools, movie stars) to South Dakota (buffalo and snow) of all places. The reason he did this (with my mom's help) was that he was given six months to live. He believed that when he died, my mother would need help raising me and my five brothers and sisters. Fortunately, my dad was an early recipient of a heart valve replacement. He lived bravely, though with health challenges, for another forty years. His health challenges didn't deter him from fighting GGB status.

We grew up in Rutland, South Dakota, which had a population of fifty people—FIVE-ZERO people. It was a great place to grow up. We did everything, including being active in many sports. It was one of these sports that solidified in my mind that my dad had vision. He looked at possibility while living in reality.

We didn't have a baseball field in Rutland, so even if we could field a team (which was difficult due to the low population and dependence upon farm kids), every game would be an away game. Playing away games all the time didn't make sense to my dad. He decided to see what wasn't and make it real. Somehow, he convinced the school board to allow a baseball field to be built across the football field. He made numerous calls to secure the materials needed. He had no money to contribute to the noble cause. What he did have was a desire to see his son play a home game.

He needed giant poles to form the backstop. He got them. He needed wire fence to put on the poles to complete the backstop and he obtained that as well. A pitching mound had to be created by hauling in more dirt.

Obtaining the needed supplies was only part of the equation. Similar to life, gaining knowledge and supplies is not enough. Knowledge is not power. Applied knowledge is power. It is not enough to simply know what to do. You must act on the information.

So he had to apply determination to solicit free help to erect the first and only baseball field in Rutland, SD. All of that took an immense amount of energy, which was not something my dad possessed in abundance. His health was a constant challenge. Somehow, with great assistance, the field was completed. We then needed a team. He made calls to field a team to play with me. Then we needed to look like a team, so he convinced a Pepsi distributor to donate t-shirts.

Guess who coached us? We weren't very good, but we played home games with matching t-shirts.

Did we have a baseball field? No. Did we have money? No. Did we have uniforms? No. What did we have? We had one man with tremendous desire. He said, "Don't tell me no; tell me how."

He heard "no," but figured out "how." He knew there was no talent in complaining. The real talent is finding solutions.

You have to stop being a GGB because it's really hard to continue ignoring the opportunities around you. You don't see them? If you don't, you're probably focused too much on reality and not enough on possibility.

You have to stop being a GGB because there are too many opportunities. They're all over the place…just look…with your eyes shut.

It's harder to envision overcoming hurdles when you're staring at them. When we close our eyes, we can see ourselves doing amazing things. Reality is temporary. You can change it. Don't let it get in the way and become an excuse.

Most importantly, you owe it to God. Don't cheat God. The penalty must be severe. God took time to create you in a manner that allows you the freedom to choose and that means you do not have to become a GGB.

You're cheating yourself if you are a GGB. You're not getting everything you can out of the physical, spiritual, and mental gifts you possess. You owe it to yourself to stop being a GGB. There is more *you* to you, and you know it, don't you? (That is my personal record for the use of "you" in one sentence.) You owe it to your family, siblings, parents, neighbors, and even strangers.

You're not using your mind if you are a GGB. An old advertisement on television (back in the day when people watched commercials) said, "A mind is a terrible thing to waste." Are you getting the most out of yours? Sure? Many people think that knowledge is power. That is untrue. Applied knowledge is power. Descartes said it best, "It is not enough to have a good mind; the main thing is to use it well."

You weren't designed for mediocrity. You aren't wired for apathy and the resulting melancholy. You are an amazing being.

The human body is comprised of one hundred trillion cells, 206 bones, and over 350 muscles; and the brain is comprised of billions of neurons.

Each human has all of that, including you. Yet, we're all unique, so unique that we don't have to think, act, behave and look the same…like…Green Golf Balls.

GGBs cheat many people, mostly themselves. GGBs think of many reasons why they can't or won't change. All they really need is one powerful reason why they can—just one. But, the more reasons for achieving your goals the better and more powerful you will change.

WHY YOU HAVE TO STOP BEING ONE

➤ You're cheating yourself.

➤ You're not using your mind.

➤ You're not designed for mediocrity.

➤ You owe it to your children.

➤ It's hard to continue being a GGB.

➤ There are too many opportunities available.

➤ You owe it to God.

Summary

Tee these up!

One thing I will stop doing after reading this chapter to help me stop my GGB route:

One thing I will continue to do after reading this chapter to stop my GGB route:

One thing I will start doing after reading this chapter that will change my GGB route:

CHAPTER 4

Who Can Help If You Are One

To change the world takes time; to change yourself takes courage.

R.S. Lowel

A few years ago, my left knee sent a message that it was not feeling well. It became swollen after some minor physical activity. It persisted, so I went to a doctor, who ordered an x-ray and then an MRI. The doctor discovered that years of physical activity and a high school football injury had deteriorated the cartilage in my left knee. He said I was a very young candidate for a knee replacement, but was quickly heading that way. His advice was not to run (Good! I never was a runner) and to limit the impact on my knee.

The next day, I bought running shoes and became a runner. I decided that if I needed a new knee I would get every mile out of the one God gave me. This was an empowering decision that I'll never regret. My left knee feels great and still works fine.

The first person that can help you if you're a GGB is you. Admit that you are a GGB, or at least have GGB traits. You can only control your attitude and effort. Attitude and effort are EVERYTHING you need to become great and shed your green sheen.

You can make decisions like that. *You* can help you if you're a GGB.

Other people who can (and likely will) help if you're a GGB are those that aren't GGBs. Identify them. Here's how.

- Whom do you admire?

- Why do you admire them?

- Who is a leader in your life?

- Who is a leader at work?

- Who makes the amount of money you desire?

- Who has the job you covet?

- Who is in the physical shape you want?

So what if they're strangers. If you reach out to them, the worst thing that can happen is they'll be flattered that you think they're not a GGB. The best thing that can happen is that they'll share wisdom on their success and offer to help you shed your GGB status. Let them know you don't want to be a GGB, and they're likely to help. Does this seem like an unreasonable or rare response from a stranger? It is. That's what makes them winners, leaders, and successes. They're willing to share. If not, they may be a GGB, or worse.

God has guided me, lifted me, taught me, and blessed me by keeping me from becoming a GGB. It takes courage. I figured out that God supplied the courage and I could add my attitude and effort to succeed. It's that simple.

Friends, real friends, real non-judgmental friends will help you if you're becoming or became a GGB. Let them know what you're trying to accomplish and share your specific goals. This is a good test to see if they're willing to help and show their friendship. False friends, fleeting friends will resent your desire to move away from the herd piled at the top of the bell curve.

Family members can be powerful allies in your pursuit of change. Some family members, however, may resent your desire to improve. They may take it personally and feel that your pursuit is an indictment of their place in life and role as a GGB. Don't let them bring you down.

"The bond that links your true family is not one of blood, but of respect and joy in each other's life. Rarely do members of one family grow up under the same roof" (Richard Bach, *Illusions*).

Most of the limitations you currently face were self-fabricated. In this real world, there are boundaries, and you erected most of them. In order to break them down, you must want to shatter them AND believe it's possible. In your imagination, everything is possible. Your powerful mind can bridge the gap between imagination (where anything is possible) to reality (where you'll make it probable). The power to stop being a GGB can come from many sources. First, imagine it done and seek help. Then…it will be done.

WHO CAN HELP IF YOU ARE ONE

➤ You

➤ Others—non GGBs

➤ God

➤ Friends

➤ Family

Summary

Tee these up!

One person I will stop communicating with after reading this chapter:

One person I will continue to meet after reading this chapter:

One person I will start meeting with after reading this chapter:

CHAPTER 5

What to Do When You're Turning Green

Change your life today. Don't gamble on the future, act now, without delay.

Simone De Beauvoir

If you're green or turning green, you may need mental triggers to spur you on to drop the GGB status. An autographed baseball is a reminder to me to take time to work out, eat right, and exercise discipline. Who signed the baseball? You may think it must be someone in the Baseball Hall-of-Fame. You may think it's someone that fans worship and adore. You would be wrong. The autographed baseball that serves as a mental trigger for me was signed by my dad in the last week of his life. Somehow, God guided me to ask him to autograph a baseball. It sits on my bathroom counter and I see it every day and every night when I'm not traveling. That baseball reminds me to laugh, learn, and do more. The message it sends the loudest is not to take anything for granted, especially those things you can affect. There are mornings when I wake up tired and sore, and perhaps feeling sorry for myself. I see that baseball and realize how strong my dad must have been to endure his health challenges. He must have felt worse, so I suck it up and carpe diem. There are other times when I return home after a long day at work and feel exhausted. All I have to do is catch a glimpse of that ball and my energy is restored.

So what can you do when you're turning green? Seek inspiration from the strength of others, alter your routine and attach many reasons (whys) to what you want to do. The more positive reasons to do something the more likely you'll succeed.

You must understand the value of time if you're turning green. Every person everywhere has the same number of minutes and hours in each day. They are not guaranteed, but God willing, they're yours to spend as you wish.

You may want to try a few things. None of them are foolproof, and you may not agree with some of them. The point is that you must try something.

Ask your most free-spirited, adventurous friend or acquaintance what he/she would do. The response is likely to be outside (or way outside) of your comfort zone. The point is to get another perspective and one that is not going to appear safe or average. GGBs are safe and average. Safe and average contributed to your GGB persona.

Go against your traditional instinct. Assess the situation and clearly write down what your first instinct is. What are you most likely to do? Then do something else. Habit, tradition, conformity, and repetition got you there. Something needs to change and break the pattern.

Change. If you want your life to change, you must take action to change it. Of all the events that have occurred in your life, there is only one common denominator—you. You were there when you didn't study hard enough. It was you that didn't give your employer a full day of work. You ended up where you are, so YOU must initiate change.

And change will take this path…pay attention. First, you'll tell yourself it will be easy. After all, so many other people have done what you want to do. At this stage, you'll be confident and full of naive optimism. Then you'll discover it's harder than what you first thought. It hurts more than you imagined. Change is not easy, but it's possible. Nobody told you it would be this hard. Reality has set in. It is at this point that you'll be tempted to quit. Most people do. Most people are GGBs, but you won't quit for two reasons. First, I have warned you that this was coming. To be forewarned is to be prepared. If you know the clouds are coming, you can bring an umbrella. They're coming because change is not easy.

The main reason you won't quit is because prior to starting this process, you listed WHY you want to change. And you listed many reasons.

Some of these reasons will be to avoid pain and others will be to seek pleasure—"It will feel great when…" or "I don't want to keep buying bigger clothes." Make sure you have some pleasure seeking and pain avoiding reasons. Know your motivators. This is when you should revisit your written list.

These reasons will fill in the danger gap between "This is harder than I thought" and "It looks like I'm doing this."

When you have made it to the "It looks like I'm doing this" stage, your confidence is building. Optimism grows. You may even be inspiring others without knowing it. At this stage of change, your inner dialog changes. You start to say, "I am doing this." And continue to change.

Finally, you get to the stage described by philosopher Flintstone as the "Yabba Dabba Do" moment. You did it. You changed.

Re-assess your goals. GGBs rarely commit them to writing, but a written goal is more likely to be achieved. Let's pretend you have goals. Did you hit them? Were they too easy? Too hard? Did you attach enough "whys" to them?

*"He who has a **why** to live can bear almost any **how**"* (Friedrich Nietzsche).

Then…start over with new goals. Make sure they're goals and not wishes. Make sure you believe they are attainable. Really, deeply, passionately believe in yourself and your goals. Then for each goal, add five whys.

EXAMPLE

Run a half marathon by December 31.

Why? Set an example for my kids.

Why? So my kids will they'll know running 13.1 miles is possible.

Why? So my children will be encouraged to work out.

Why? So my family will pursue a a longer, healthier life.

Why? So they can maximize their potential and be an example for their children.

How much could you do in 86,400 seconds? That's how many there are in each day. The person that spends them wisely and understands their value is not a GGB.

The following people had 86,400 seconds in their day:

Abraham Lincoln	Oskar Schindler
Mother Teresa	Henry Aaron
Larry Bird	Bill Gates
Martin Luther King	Helen Keller
Jackie Robinson	Ralph Waldo Emerson
Winston Churchill	Nelson Mandela
Wolfgang Mozart	Eleanor Roosevelt

Dr. Micheal A. Clark is not a GGB. He has spent every second of his life wisely. So wisely that he is the physical therapist for the Phoenix Suns, is the president of the National Academy of Sports Medicine, was named "Health and Fitness Visionary of the Year" for 2005 by *Men's Health* magazine, was credited by Shaquille O'Neal for putting him back together and resurrecting his career and status as a NBA All-Star, serves on the advisory board for Lance Armstrong's Livestrong Foundation, created Optimum Performance Training, is the father of three beautiful daughters, and is a loving husband.

He has the same number of seconds to spend each day as you do. How can he do all this? Because he wants to. Why does he do this? Because it makes a difference in the lives of others. He doesn't do all of this because he's super-human or because he has to. He does it because he chooses to. He chooses not to be a GGB. What are you choosing?

WHAT TO DO WHEN YOU'RE TURNING GREEN

➤ Ask a free-spirited friend what he/she would do.

➤ Go against your traditional instincts.

➤ Change.

- o "This will be easy."

- o "This is harder than I thought."

- o DANGER—what are your motivators?

- o "It looks like I'm doing this."

- o "I am doing this."

- o "Yabba Dabba Do—I did it!"

➤ Use mental triggers.

➤ Value time.

Summary

Tee these up!

One thing I will stop doing when I am turning green after reading this chapter:

One thing I will continue to do when I am turning green after reading this chapter:

One thing I will start doing when I am turning green after reading this chapter:

CHAPTER 6

How to Stop Friends and Family from Becoming One

Act as if what you do makes a difference. It does.

William James

There are ten ways to stop friends and family from becoming GGBs.

    1.   Don't be one.

You can be an example, and that can be good or bad. It comes down to choices. Are you setting a good example? Do you understand the two pains in life (see Chapter 1)? The result will be that people become leaders because of you and not simply followers.

    2.   Live every day—carpe diem.

There are 86,400 seconds in a day. I'll always remember the person that taught me that. Thanks Mike. The people that spend these precious seconds wisely are the happiest. They are also not GGBs.

    3.   Set goals.

The first thing to understand regarding goals is what they are. What is your definition? A simple way to define a goal is to say that it's something you're willing to work for. Earl Nightingale said that a goal is a "progressive realization of a worthy ideal."

Before you set a goal, you need to know what one is and what one isn't. It isn't a wish or a general desire. "I want to win the lottery" is a wish, not a goal. In order for something to be a goal, you need to have a majority of the influence in whether it is achieved…or not. You have options. And the coolest thing about goals is that you choose them. You have choices, but choices are inert and factual. Not everybody is motivated by facts. Emotion causes more success and failure than anything in the world. Choices are the precursor to decisions, which cause action or inaction. Decisions are emotional and choices are factual.

This is the primary reason some people succeed and others don't. Winners know that goals are formed and achieved in four ways. The first time a goal is formed is when you create a mental picture of what you want or what you want to accomplish. Let's says you want to climb a mountain. You must envision yourself on top of the mountain. You can see for miles. The sky is blue and the air is fresh. You can feel the wind. Use all of your senses to feel yourself on the summit.

The second time a goal is formed is when you write it down. Many dreams, visions, and goals die on the vine because the GGBs rarely write down their goals. They dream, but that's as far as it goes.

The third time a goal is formed is when you say it. "I am going to climb a mountain." Even better is, "I am going to climb Mt. Whitney in July." There is psychological power in a specific verbal commitment.

The final and most important time a goal takes shape is when you TAKE ACTION! You may have formed a mental picture, written down the goal, and even said it out loud, but unless you take action, you'll remain a GGB. All four things must happen for a goal to be realized. Then…set another goal…then another… and repeat.

4. Be adventurous.

   A GGB may take risks and seek adventure, but they're generally not well calculated and often they end up as total failures. In general though, GGBs don't venture outside of a comfort zone narrower than most. If you want to keep friends and family from the water hazard of mediocrity or worse, you need to be an example. I was born in Denver, so perhaps the mountains are in my blood. They also fuel my desire for adventure, so each summer my goal is to summit another peak. Do you take intelligent chances? Do you share successes and failures?

5. Put more of *you* in you. Be more YOU!

   Do you maximize your opportunities? Are you cheating yourself? There may be something you deeply think you would enjoy or be good at, but you haven't pursued it. Only you know what it is. Share that vision with people you trust, and they'll share theirs. Becoming more comfortable with yourself puts others at ease and frees them to pursue their dreams, potential, and passions.

6. Learn.

   This has been called the information age. By simply reading this book, you're shedding GGB tendencies and pursuing knowledge. A lifetime of learning and encouraging others to do the same is a great way (perhaps the best) to keep friends and family from becoming GGBs.

One great way to learn is to listen. Listening to yourself may be liberating. It has been said that the loudest noise in the world is silence. I didn't understand that for long time. It was only when I realized that many people (and all GGBs) fill silence with negative dialog. What are they looking at? Is something hanging out of my nose? Is my zipper down? What are they thinking? Do they like me? Do they think I'm ugly?

See how it's easy to fill silence with negative self-talk? Words matter, and the words you use with yourself matter most. Listening to others is an effective learning methodology. Don't simply wait to listen to whomever you encounter. A Green Golf Ball would do that. Seek opportunities to listen to experts. Even if you dislike or disagree with the speaker, you can learn. What is their delivery style? Is there something you can learn from that? If you're blessed to have your parents living, you must stop reading now and seek them out for knowledge. I did that and cherish the result.

The most important listening I've done lately was in response to a request. I asked my mom to list what she has learned in her twenty-nine years on earth. I know…odd for her to be so young.

She titled it, "31 Things I've Learned in 23 ¾ Years."

She claimed to be 23 ¾ after every birthday. Here is her list. I've learned…

1. To thank God every morning for the new day and whatever it will bring
2. To love unconditionally
3. To hate no one
4. To hold no grudges and to forgive
5. To accept people for who they are and not for what you want them to be
6. To look for the good in everyone
7. That out of every bad situation, good can come if you really look for it
8. That you can learn from your mistakes and to recognize and admit your mistakes, even if just to yourself
9. That if you develop a love of reading, you will never be lonely—books are great friends

10. To not believe everything you see or hear—especially on TV, radio, or newspapers

11. <u>Not</u> to run outside when it's <u>15 degrees below</u> zero in my <u>socks</u>—no shoes—to take a picture of fresh, beautiful snow on pine trees at sunrise

12. To appreciate the beauty in nature and take time to enjoy it.

13. To be careful changing a baby boy—if you aren't, you could be in for a surprise

14. To never walk in the dark in a strange place—it can be hazardous to your health, especially when you stumble and fall…Ouch!

15. How wonderful it is, and the magic of, playing with a granddaughter in the sand or drawing on the sidewalk with chalk

16. You can learn a lot from a child, also your pet dog—enjoy the simple things

17. The joy of work and doing a good job, and the feeling of gratification when it is done—without work, life is nothing

18. That God makes miracles, even in this day and age

19. That a hot fudge sundae is the best way of curing the blues

20. Always to wear clean underwear. You never know when you might have an accident or get sick (Heaven forbid!)

21. To, finally, put off until tomorrow or the next day what doesn't need to be done today

22. Not to feel guilty about mistakes I've made and vow not to make them again, and do better in the future

23. I can overcome adverse events and not let them rule my life; they can make you a better person… get over it!!

24. To be a gracious recipient; it makes the giver feel good and is the most important thing in receiving—even if it is something you don't need, advice, or something you can do for yourself (I learned this a long time ago; my mother told me this.)
25. Always be prepared, as the Boy Scouts say—be prepared for anything and everything

Additional things I've learned…

1. Chocolate rules!
2. Money isn't everything—but it sure helps.
3. Never trust a redhead with twinkling blue eyes, a mischievous grin, and yellow shirt. You may have to spend fifty-four years, eight months, and twenty-seven days with him.
4. To depend on myself—I can do anything!
5. To thank God for my wonderful life
6. Last but not least, <u>I Am Still Learning!!!!!</u>

   So my mother actually provided thirty-one things. She is always doing more than expected. I love her and she is not a GGB in any way, shape, or form.
7. Teach.
   You've learned. Now teach. It's an obligation if you want to prevent friends and family from a sad existence. There are three levels of learning. The first level is to learn enough to pass a test. The second level is to learn enough to apply the knowledge. The third level is to learn deeply enough to be able to teach what you've learned.

8. Encourage dreams.

I grew up with three brothers and four sisters. Amazingly, our parents made each of us feel like we were their favorite child. They encouraged us, taught us, and implored us to seek what made us happy. My mom, in particular, fostered the belief that anything was possible. She told me numerous times that I could do anything in the world, go anywhere in the world, and become anything I wanted. As a kid interested in many things, this made my childhood rewarding and interesting. In the fall, I wanted to be a professional football player. In the spring and summer, I wanted to be Hank Aaron and break his home run record each year. The winter created one of my favorite memories. Winters in South Dakota can be harsh, and often are brutal with frequent blizzards. Our driveway was dirt, and as it rained, snowed, and froze, deep ruts formed, making it difficult to dribble a basketball. But this was the only court available.

One cold day, as I shoveled our driveway/basketball court, my destiny appeared. It was about ten degrees (which was a warm day), and with each shovel of snow, my future gradually came in focus. I dropped the shovel and ran into the house as fast as my nine-year-old legs laden with snow pants could carry me. I took off my boots, hat, coat, gloves, another coat, sweatshirt, and yet another coat as I yelled, "Mom!" She was drinking coffee at the kitchen table so I sat down.

"Mom, remember how you told me I could do anything…that I could even be president if I wanted? Well I know what I want to be when I grow up." She took a sip of coffee and asked what I wanted to be.

"I figured it out when I was shoveling so I could shoot baskets. I AM GOING TO PLAY FOR THE HAR-LEM GLOBETROTTERS!"

At that moment, my mother could have been a dream killer. She could have told me I would never play for the Harlem Globetrotters. She could have been brutally honest. She also could have said it would be unlikely I would ever be good enough to play for them, that I just wouldn't have the ability. She could have simply said, "Isn't that nice." A GGB parent would have probably said any one of those things. And their negative message would have been delivered in a negative manner. "You'll never be good enough. You're the wrong color. Give it up." What would you have done if you were my mother? What would you have said to a nine-year-old kid with a delusional dream?

She said, "In order to play for the Globetrotters, you need to be a great basketball player. It takes a lot of practice to be great at anything, so you'll need to practice that way." My mother would not kill this dream, as she knew time and circumstances would dissolve it anyway. I didn't know I couldn't do it and she wasn't about to tell me. I sprinted back outside and practiced a lot. I never did make it.

A GGB parent would have killed that dream and probably all others, even if they were reasonable.

9. Encourage unique traits.
    Do you recognize, appreciate, and respect the dif-ferences in your friends and family? Do you com-

pliment them when they try something, even if it doesn't work out?

10. Reward and praise success.

Catch people doing the right things. Reward them and encourage them to set new goals. Help them understand that they should only look back to learn, and never to regret. They should look back to remember past success to fuel future growth. NEVER ever let them look back and regret. When you catch someone rewinding their lives and making statements like, "I shouldn't have done that" or "I wish I could re-do that" or "I'm sorry it turned out that way," stop them from doing that, and remind them of what they have done successfully.

Pay close attention to the words you use to friends and family when you're attempting to encourage them and recognize success. It is amazing how changing one word can entirely alter the perception of a statement. You may mean to compliment them, but it may lack effect because of one word.

Let's say your child comes home with his/her report card. Overall, it's very good. You notice three As, one B, and a C. You may say something like, "This looks good *but* you got a C in Math." What if you said, "This looks good, *AND* when that Math grade goes up it will be amazing." Changing "but" to "and" altered the entire sentence. How would this change your perception if you had been on the receiving end? One word. That's all it takes to make a statement positive and motivating instead of negative.

HOW TO STOP FRIENDS AND FAMILY FROM BECOMING ONE

➤ Don't be one.

➤ Carpe diem.

➤ Set goals.

➤ Be adventurous.

➤ Put more of *you* into you.

➤ Learn.

➤ Teach.

➤ Encourage dreams.

➤ Encourage unique traits.

➤ Reward and praise success.

Summary

Tee these up!

One person I will stop from becoming green after reading this chapter:

One person I will continue to keep from becoming green after reading this chapter:

One person I will encourage changing from a GGB after reading this chapter:

CHAPTER 7

Green Golf Balls and Greenbacks

All wealth is the product of labor.

John Locke

"Greenbacks" are green, but they don't blend in.

Average income, average debt—don't compare yourself to average. You'll be happy simply being a lighter shade of green. That's not good enough. Beating the average only raises the average. Your goal is to stand out. How has your income grown in the last five years? It should be growing in contrast to your waistband. More importantly, your savings and investments should be growing.

The best way to make money and maintain a balanced life is to answer two questions. What am I good at? What do I like to do? If you can answer these questions and find where they overlap, you have identified the sweet spot of your life, and that's probably where you'll make the most money. God has not given any talent that can't become a career with desire.

I enjoy playing basketball, but I am not very good. I am good at landscaping, but find no pleasure in doing it. This is evidence of how the answers to these important questions may be disconnected. If I enjoyed landscaping, people would pay notice and pay me. If I was really good at basketball, there are teams all over the world in need of talent. What I'm good at (landscaping) and enjoy (playing basketball) are disconnected. One of them

I don't want to make a living doing and the other one I can't make a living doing.

Many people are doing what they're good at because it "pays the bills." As an aspiring non-GGB, you are not interested in working to simply "pay the bills." You want more than that. WAY MORE!

I am blessed to make a difference and a living doing what I enjoy *and* what I'm good at. Based on feedback, I am effective in teaching and inspiring, which brings me pleasure. My likes and abilities were identified by me early in life. Only later did I have the courage to pursue my calling where ability (what I am good at) and desire (what I like to do) intersected. I did this later in life than I wished.

It can be liberating or scary. Do it anyway. I did this at a time in my life where it was not evident what I should do. I was lost. My job was economically rewarding, but I didn't enjoy it. With each promotion, I moved farther from "the people" and closer to the boardroom and "those people." I moved from people to paper and that's not me. Asking these questions helped me find my sweet spot.

You can do it sooner, like now. Answer the questions posed earlier. *What are you good at?* Many times, it will be what gives you the most confidence and energizes you. You should also ask others what they believe you are good at. It's possible they'll see latent talents that you possess.

What do you like to do? Your answer is more important than that from someone you trust. Only *you* really know you. Do not fear if your answer would cause others to view you differently. If you really like to paint, do it. Even if others may say, "I can't see you doing that." What matters is that you see yourself doing it, because, you're going to do it. You are. Right? You're not a GGB are you?

Start painting. You're not good at it? So what? There's something you're probably blessed to do now that you don't even think about it. When you started, you were terrible. In fact, you were so bad you were hurt trying, so bad that your parents may have worried whether you would ever "get it." Repeated failures and brushes with bodily harm and pain did not discourage you. You saw others doing it and knew you could as well. Yet, you kept falling…repeatedly. You never gave up, and one day you took a wobbly step. Somehow, miraculously, your knees stayed above your feet and you walked. Probably, your first steps were in the direction of a smiling parent. You DID IT! You walked. Now you don't even think about it.

That's exactly what happens whenever we start something, unless, we're immediately good at it. Usually, in that case, we lose interest because it seems easy. You may have to take lessons to become talented at something you like to do. So what? You may have to fall down and stink at it for a while. So what? You may have to practice a lot. So what? You may never make a living at it. So what? You like to do it, and you may get so good you could be paid for it. WOW! Imagine that.

An artist was discovered in the body of a certified public accountant while watching his daughter play soccer. He was doodling to fend off boredom. Somebody noticed his drawing and asked what he did for a living. They didn't believe that he was a CPA. He just said he liked to draw. And he was very talented. At age forty, his career took a turn from what he was good at (accounting) to something he was good at *and* enjoyed (drawing). He's a wealthy artist living a life exposed by a sketch at a soccer game. The person sitting next to him at that game worked for Hallmark and recognized the immense talent blossoming in an accountant.

Let's say you have the deep conviction that what you'd like to do is something that you'll never be good enough to be paid for. You believe that in order to "pay the bills," or more, you need to stick with what you're good at whether you like it or not. There is no shame in that, unless you're miserable and it has condemned you to the GGB status in all other phases of your life.

What are you good at? I bet you can list at least ten things…
as long as one of them isn't procrastination.

1.
2.
3.
4.
5.
6.
7.
8.
9.
10.

What do you like to do? You can easily list twenty things.

1.
2.
3.
4.
5.
6.
7.
8.
9.
10.
11.
12.
13.
14.
15.
16.
17.
18.
19.
20.

Now compare the lists and identify where they overlap. It is at this intersection where you'll make the most money. However, you'll only do this if you answer those two questions honestly and evaluate the answers. You will then only need to apply your desire and pursue your destiny with faith. Sure, you'll fall down. You may even bump your head. That's an experience you have encountered many times, and you're a great walker now. It really isn't much different.

A big mistake people make is that they chase $ instead of ☺. If you chase $ you'll end up ☹. Somebody will always have bigger $.

Nobody can smile more than you. It's impossible. The best thing you can do is to find out what makes you ☺ the most, work hard to be the best at it, and the $ will find you… maybe even $$$$$$!

In the end, do you want to make a life or a living?

Caution: More money makes people more of what they already are. If they're a jerk and somehow get more money, they'll be a bigger jerk. A jerk that gets money will not suddenly become a good person. If a person is nice and gets more money, they'll be more generous. Money is a magnifier of strengths and weaknesses.

GGBs have an average or lower pile of greenbacks. That's not for you is it?

GREEN GOLF BALLS AND GREEN-BACKS

➤ Ask and answer these two questions.

    o   **What am I good at?**

    o   **What do I love to do?**

➤ Chase ☺, not $.

Summary

Tee these up!

One thing I will stop doing after reading this chapter that will lead to more money:

One thing I will continue to do after reading this chapter that will lead to more money:

One thing I will start doing after reading this chapter that will lead to more money:

CHAPTER 8

Green Golf Balls and Your Health

Health is the condition of wisdom.

Ralph Waldo Emerson

It has been said that if you have your health you have eve-rything. Like all important things in life that we get free, we take our health for granted…at least until we're not healthy. It is then that we think about how good it feels to feel good. Unfortunately, there is little we can do to change the present situation.

Some of us may have the genetic cards stacked against us. Some of us may be blessed genetically. However you're designed, you can make decisions to change. Let's say you're looking in the mirror. The person looking back has the eyes you remember seeing since youth. They may be wrapped in wrinkles but the color is what you saw as a child. You pan down and notice that somebody has replaced your youthful, spry, thin body with… something older, brittle, and thicker. That somebody is you. Many little choices YOU MADE contributed to the present (less than flattering) view. It is likely to take twice as many disciplined decisions to change what you see in the mirror. That's not hor-rible news because you have the power to make better, healthy choices.

You didn't gain twenty pounds. You gained one pound twenty times. Oddly enough, the first one you gained was the easiest. It snuck on with a few snacks and poor eating decisions. The next pound had it easier to sneak onto your body because you were slower. Each additional pound had an easier path to your body.

You're not going to lose twenty pounds either. You will lose one pound twenty times. The first one will be stubborn and the toughest. It's the hardest one to lose because it's the first one to go when you make changes and better choices. It will be belligerent, but when you lodge it free, others will follow. It wants to hang out at the cellulose beach you built on the sedentary sea. You'll gain strength as the extra weight loses its hold. As you move more each day (because of the reduced weight), it becomes easier to shed the dimpled GGB skin you developed.

Your present situation didn't happen overnight, so it won't be corrected immediately. Here is the only diet plan you will ever need.

Eat less. Move more.

That's it. Don't eat as much as you normally would. Move more than you normally would. (Most people walk less than three miles per day.) Do both of these—eat less, move more—today. Move today more than yesterday. Walk. Jog. Run. Swim. Bike. Climb. Dance. Stretch. MOVE. JUST MOVE! MOVE MORE!

Don't be discouraged if the results aren't immediately noticed. As each pound that latched on was hardly noticed so stick to it and they will disappear. All it takes is mental toughness and discipline. You'll be amazed at how much you can accomplish.

An overweight smoker from a family plagued by obesity could probably never run one block, let alone a 5k. A 10k would be unattainable, a marathon a nightmare/dream and running a hundred miles…at a time…would forever be impossible, or not. Meet Kevin Sullivan.

Kevin Sullivan competes and completes ultra-marathons. These races are one hundred miles long. It has been estimated that the average American walks about three miles per hour. Kevin runs one hundred miles in less than seventeen hours. He is clearly not a Green Golf Ball. You may want to know what he has that you don't in order to achieve this impressive physical accomplishment. He only has one thing you don't—more on that later. Kevin is slender and weighs about 145 pounds. You're not that size. In fact, you may have become golf ball shaped. You *became* that way. You aren't really that way, and aren't meant to be.

On one weekend, Kevin ran a 50k race on Saturday and a marathon on Sunday. True story. A 50k to warm up for a marathon. Crazy, huh? He must train twenty-four hours a day. Not really. He's a successful attorney.

So what you have physically (extra pounds) and mentally (bad habits) may prevent you from running a 5k, 10k, half-marathon, or even a marathon. You brought them on and you can take them off. So you're curious about what Kevin possesses that you don't? The key is not cool running shoes. It's not a runner's physique (because under your dimpled cover you have the same runner's body). It's not genetic blessing. It's simply this. Kevin believes he can do something like that and you don't. You don't have to believe you can run one hundred miles but if you believed that you could, you actually could. You really could. Kevin believes it and applies his desire. Whatever you believe is true. Change your belief and remove that green, dimpled skin.

Phillip Mann, Jr., was a freshman at DePauw University in Greencastle, IN. He played defensive back as a freshman on the football team but that career was over. He signed up for a class called "The Science of Cycling." It was in this class, at the age of nineteen, that he discovered his passion—cycling, competitive cycling. He had mountain biked in high school and was a top regional competitor. Kansas isn't the most mountainous region and that's where he lived, so he was never exposed to top-notch competition. That changed in college. He became the National Collegiate Cycling Association of the USA's national champion. Twice! And both victories followed after finishing second by the length of this book—that close. The year prior to his narrow, disappointing second place finish, he wiped out in the lead pack with only two turns left. He was devastated, but not permanently, and not enough to become a GGB.

He graduated from Colorado State University and earned a Masters Degree in Health and Nutrition. Academically and athletically, he was never a GGB. People that excel in one area of life are often not GGBs in other aspects of life.

Your physical and mental health is the foundation for your success. Investing a few of the minutes of discretionary time and effort you possess each day in physical activity is a great use of you.

GREEN GOLF BALLS AND YOUR HEALTH

➤ Eat less.

➤ Move more.

Summary

Tee these up!

One thing I will stop eating after reading this chapter:

One exercise I will continue to do after reading this chapter:

One activity I will start doing after reading this chapter:

CHAPTER 9

How to Stop Being One at Work

The tougher the job, the greater the reward.

George Allen

Many people are disgruntled. Only a few are gruntled… whatever that means. Primarily they're interested in making more money and smiling more. Unfortunately, they believe these two areas are directly connected in that order. Many studies have determined, however, that smiling first leads to more money and not the other way around.

A majority of unhappy people and GGBs would rather show their displeasure (vocally or by activity or inactivity) than change the situation. For some people, complaining is therapy. Seeking solutions, in their warped world, would diminish the value of the self-ascribed therapy. In summary, it's easier to complain than do something about it.

The formula most people desire is:

$$\frac{\text{Smile} + \$ + \text{ZZZZ}}{\text{Time}}$$

We want to be happy, make money, and sleep. And we want to do this over an extended period of time. Even GGBs want this. That's what we all want, but we don't always know how to do it.

So how do we accomplish this? Very simply: Do more. This is easy to say and remarkably even easier to execute.

What does "do more" mean?

What if you were a salesperson and made just one more phone call each day? That would amount over two hundred additional calls per year. Would that increase sales?

What if you thanked someone personally every day? Would your reputation as a caring professional be enhanced?

What if you sent just one handwritten thank-you note each week? Would fifty-two people be impressed? What would impressing fifty-two people each year do for your reputation? How do you feel when you think about the last personal, hand-written note you received?

What if you spent just one more minute with customers and prospects asking them if there was anything else they needed to make their job easier? Just one minute. Would that impress them and increase your job satisfaction?

What if you waited just fifteen seconds to hold the door for someone? What would they think of you? What would you think if someone did that for you?

What if the time you spent watching television was spent reading? Would you learn more? Would that knowledge help you in your career? What if you changed what you watched on television? What if you watched the History Channel instead of MTV? A biography versus some inane real life "drama"?

What if the time you spent watching television was spent in a real conversation with your family? Could you ever measure the positive return on investment generated by that?

What if you called a friend instead of sending an e-mail? What if you wrote a note to thank a teacher that influenced you in a positive way?

It has been said that we become that we think about. Why not think about becoming the person that is known for giving more.

Are you the first one in the office? The last to leave? Do you smile more than anyone? Do you ask for more work?

Doing more always feels good. It doesn't always mean you'll win. But as legendary football coach Vince Lombardi said, "The price of success is hard work, dedication to the job at hand, and the determination that whether we win or lose, we have applied the best of ourselves to the task at hand."

Being in the present, applying ourselves to the task at hand, and doing more to *create* success. When someone comes to your office to talk, do you look at your computer? Do you check e-mail? Are you giving them attention or passing time until they leave?

This chapter has included thirty-one questions so far. Ask and honestly answer every one of them and you're likely to identify areas for immediate improvement. Do you have the courage to address an area of deficiency? Do you possess the discipline? If you attach at least two positive reasons for doing any of these things, you'll move closer to full "gruntlement." Adios disgruntlement! You'll no longer be a GGB and you'll feel great.

A few people will read this and begin lamenting about the times they failed to do any of these things. They will look back, realize they could have done more, and feel remorse or regret. They will look in a mirror, and the reflection will be green. I caution you not to do that, but if you choose this path, make it fast. Get over it. Only look back to learn, not regret.

So what is the best way to stop being a Green Golf Ball at work and make more money, and increase happiness and sleep? Two words: Do more.

HOW TO STOP BEING ONE AT WORK

➤ Do more.

➤ Complain less or leave.

Summary

Tee these up!

One thing I will stop doing at work after reading this chapter:

One thing I will continue to do at work after reading this chapter:

One thing I will start doing more at work after reading this chapter:

CHAPTER 10

Where and When It's OK to Be One

Life's not about fitting in; it's about standing out.

Anonymous

A scenario in which blending in may be important reminds me of one of the most inspirational people I've ever heard about. Rocky Versace. His brother, Dick, is more famous for his basketball coaching and broadcasting exposure. Rocky, however, died in captivity as a prisoner of war in Vietnam. So how did he become inspirational, other than his service to the United States and you and me? Rocky Versace wore Army green, but he was not a GGB. As a soldier, he was exemplary. As a prisoner of war, he was defiant.

Rocky was captured two weeks prior to ending his second tour of duty. He had no desire to blend in. He tried to escape at least four times. Fellow prisoners quickly realized he was not a GGB. The North Vietnamese may have wanted to send him back to his fellow soldiers if he promised never to return. He ended up tormenting them continuously while he exhibited amazing mental and physical resilience. He was committed to his Catholic faith, which provided the strength only God can. Also, as a West Point graduate, he lived the motto of "Duty, Honor, Country."

Rocky was awarded the Congressional Medal of Honor, although he died in captivity. This prestigious honor was earned because of what he did to relieve the pressure on fellow prisoners. He could speak numerous languages and would tell the captors to go to hell in all of them. This forced the North

Vietnamese to spend more time guarding him, which lessened the stress on his fellow soldiers. Rocky Versace was last seen being dragged through the jungle. At the top of his lungs, he was singing God Bless America.

Unless you're an America hero like Rocky Versace, there are times you may want to blend in, seek the top of the bell curve, and be a GGB. However, you're unlikely to find yourself in these situations often.

There are a few places to blend in, not stand out, fly below the radar, and become a GGB…temporarily. Here are the acceptable circumstances to be a GGB.

You're behind the wheel of your dream automobile. You've earned the privilege to drive this car because you're not a GGB. It's a seventy-degree day, the sun is shining, and you may have the top down if your dream car is a convertible. A great song is playing on your stereo and everything feels right. So right that your mind drifts back to the days when you wore youthful clothes. This temporary emotional vacation has created a heavy foot. You're speeding. Not good. Not good because a highway patrol officer is sitting at the side of the road with a radar gun pointed at you…or maybe one of the other cars breaking the law. You have dodged a ticket because you were blending in with the other cars and assimilating their speed. That is one situation where standing out can be costly and it is wise to be a GGB.

You're behind the wheel of a non-descript, boring, American made car. Ahead of you is another car identical to yours. Behind you is another one in a different color. You check the rear view mirror as you simultaneously monitor a long, black, chauffeur-driven limousine ahead of you. It turns right one block ahead. As you near the intersection, you determine it's OK to also turn right. It's your job to fit in, blend in, and become indistinguishable. They park. You park. Somebody gets out of the limousine so you exit your car. The person walks through a crowd and enters a bank. You're not noticed because you dress similar to most of the people on the street. The person exits the bank walking quickly and returns to the limo. You walk to your car and tail the suspect as they drive off. The chase continues. Imagine that same scene only this time you're wearing a bright blue dress with yellow flowers. You also have a purple football helmet wedged on your head. Your car is painted like a tiger on the front half and has red flames painted on the trunk. If you're a spy, it's ok to blend in and not be a GGB.

In another life, you have been turned into a leaf butterfly. You love being a leaf butterfly. You have plenty of food and more friends than you imagined. Granted, they all look like you, but at least you're beautiful. Generally, you show off your beautiful, iridescent wings. In fact, your entire life is beautiful with one exception. You are one tasty creature. At least that's what some birds think. It is the mission of a mean predator to find, kill, and eat you and a few of your beautiful, tasty friends. You don't feel like boxing up your stuff, moving, and making new friends, so you need a plan. You like it here. You and your buddies, with God's helpful design, have a defense. If a predator can't see you, they can't find, kill, and eat you, can they? As a bad guy approaches your wings, you disappear and blend into the background. The big, bad predator thinks you're a leaf, and leaves are not on his diet. You can pull this off because every bit of your body is designed to blend in. Your wings change according to the seasons. The amber veins in your wings fool the predator into thinking you're a leaf. You are beautiful when you want to be and a GGB when you have to be. It's powerful to be adaptable and may save your life.

WHERE AND WHEN IT'S OK TO BE ONE

➤ When you're speeding

➤ When you're spying

➤ When a predator is around

➤ When you're a prisoner of war

Summary

Tee these up!

One thing I will stop doing after reading this chapter:

One thing I will continue to do after reading this chapter:

One thing I will start doing after reading this chapter:

SUMMARY

At the beginning of this book, I posed this question regarding Green Golf Balls. Why aren't there any? The answer is simple. There shouldn't be any. Nobody has been made to be average.

HOW TO FIND OUT IF YOU ARE ONE

➤ Ask questions and answer them honestly.

➤ Look ahead—what do you want written on your tombstone?

HOW YOU MAY HAVE BECOME ONE

➤ You selected the wrong role models.

➤ You are in a family of them.

➤ You have made poor choices.

➤ The stigma of failure has conquered you.

➤ You have a lack of resiliency.

WHY YOU HAVE TO STOP BEING ONE

➤ You're cheating yourself.

➤ You're not using your mind.

➤ You're not designed for mediocrity.

- ➤ You owe it to your children.

- ➤ It's hard to continue being a GGB.

- ➤ There are too many opportunities available.

- ➤ You owe it to God.

WHO CAN HELP IF YOU ARE ONE

- ➤ You

- ➤ Others—non GGBs

- ➤ God

- ➤ Friends

- ➤ Family

WHAT TO DO WHEN YOU'RE TURNING GREEN

- ➤ Ask a free-spirited friend what he/she would do.

- ➤ Go against your traditional instincts.

- ➤ Change.

  - o "This will be easy."

  - o "This is harder than I thought."

o   DANGER—what are your motivators?

o   "It looks like I'm doing this."

o   "I am doing this."

o   "Yabba Dabba Do—I did it!"

➤ Use mental triggers.

➤ Value time.

HOW TO STOP FRIENDS AND FAMILY FROM BECOMING ONE

➤ Don't be one.

➤ Carpe diem.

➤ Set goals.

➤ Be adventurous.

➤ Put more of you into you.

➤ Learn.

➤ Teach.

➤ Encourage dreams.

➤ Encourage unique traits.

➤ Reward and praise success.

GREEN GOLF BALLS AND GREEN BACKS

➤ Ask and answer these two questions.

- o **What am I good at?**

- o **What do I love to do?**

➤ Chase ☺, not $.

GREEN GOLF BALLS AND YOUR HEALTH

➤ Eat less.

➤ Move more.

HOW TO STOP BEING ONE AT WORK

➤ Do more.

➤ Complain less or leave.

WHERE AND WHEN IT'S OK TO BE ONE

➤ When you're speeding

➤ When you're spying

➤ When a predator is around

➤ When you're a prisoner of war

NOT GREEN GOLF BALLS

Mary	Parker
Lindsey	Tyler
Madison	Morgan
Lucille Schoepf	Bill Schoepf
David Saben	Elizabeth Wallace
Mike Lynch	Scott Novorr
Adrien Lewis	Chuck Duske
Jason Bandy	Bob Cole
Steve Fredette	Joe McCormick
Cary Jackson	Phil Mann, Sr.
Tom Main	Vince Schaefer
Tyson Needham	Thom Hamacher
Me	You

SPECIAL THANKS
Dr. Dawn Clayton
She read this transcript and made changes that made it readable. She is an amazing person.

You can do great things wherever you are.

Adrien Lewis

ABOUT THE AUTHOR

Dan L. Schoepf grew up in South Dakota and currently lives with his wife Mary in Prairie Village, KS. He describes his children as follows:

Parker— He is one of the fairest people I know.

Lindsey—She is one of the most adventurous people I know.

Tyler—He is one of the smartest and funniest people I know.

Morgan—She is one of the most driven, dedicated people I know.

Madison—She is one of the most inspirational people I know.

You may e-mail Dan at: dan@prospectstopartners.com

18102533R00062

Made in the USA
San Bernardino, CA
29 December 2014